Tradeston to Govan in the 70s
Peter Mortimer and Duncan McCallum

At 80 Commerce Street stood Kingston U.F. Church built in 1844 to a design by D. Cousin. It had a relatively short life as a place of worship, as it was dissolved by the General Assembly in 1884, with the property being sold for £1200. The cash going towards the cost of building White Memorial Church in Paisley Road. The building was then used as commercial premises, and by the 1960s was occupied by Buchanan Bros. Ltd., who manufactured pressure gauges and thermometers. The taller building to the left was built in 1878 for William Gillespie, and was later the premises of H. Churchill & Sons, pram manufacturers. Tradeston was a busy centre for small manufacturing businesses.

Standing at the corner of Commerce Street and Kingston Street stood Tradeston Free Church, built in 1844, later known as Tradeston Gaelic Church. Like the nearby Kingston U.F. Church it ceased to operate as a church, and by 1911, had become commercial premises, indicating a depopulation of the Tradeston area, and a growth in commercial activity in the district. By the late 1920s the former church was known as the Sunlight Chambers, and was used by Lever Bros. Ltd., soap manufacturers. When this photograph was taken in September 1973 the church was in use as a clothing cash and carry. To the left, just beyond the tenement a McEwan's sign marks the spot of a much named public house. It has been variously known over the years as The Musketeers, Little Brown Jug, The Diadem, The Back Page, Standard Enquirer and the Weigh Inn.

© Peter Mortimer & Duncan McCallum, 2016
First published in the United Kingdom, 2016,
by Stenlake Publishing Ltd.
01290 551122
www.stenlake.co.uk
ISBN 9781840337662

The publishers regret that they cannot supply copies of any pictures featured in this book.

Printed by
Blissetts, Unit 1 Shield Drive,
West Cross Industrial Park, Brentford, TW8 9EX

Duncan McCallum's photographs

As Glasgow underwent massive change in the 1960s and 70s, the districts on the south bank of the Clyde suffered considerably. In the early 1970s Duncan McCallum walked about Tradeston, Kinning Park, Ibrox and Govan capturing on film this period of change.

Acknowledgements

Norrie McNamee, Alastair Callaghan, John Gorevan

Bibliograpy

The Glasgow Encyclopedia by Joe Fisher
The Industrial Archaeology of Glasgow by John Hume
The Buildings of Glasgow by Williamson, Riches & Higgs

Webpages

www.theglasgowstory.org.uk
www.scottisharchitects.org.uk
www.oldglasgowpubs.co.uk

This impressive commercial building at the corner of Clyde Place and West Street was well positioned to pick up trade from marine traffic on the River Clyde. Sadly, by the time this photograph was taken, in June 1975, it was falling into disrepair. Occupants over the years included Murray McVinnie Ltd., ships chandlers and Henry & Wright, sail-makers. The Ceilidh public house in Clyde Place looks rather lonely in its commercial surrounds, whilst the Kingston Grain Mills further along West Street remain imposing.

Facing page: The dominant two storey building in the centre was built as a confectionery works in 1884 for R. Montgomery. It was later acquired as the Scottish Offices of the Co-operative Union and became known as the Co-operative Memorial Building. A plaque above the door acknowledges workers who fell during the Great War. To the right of this image is the Camphill U.F. Church Mission, seen here in the ownership of builders' merchants Ramage, Whitehead & Co. To the extreme left are the garage premises of Melvin Motor Co., opened in 1947, who appear to be acting as Humber agents at this time. The site is now occupied by a cash and carry warehouse.

This is the ornate Kingston Grain Mills, built in 1876 for John Lamb, miller and grain merchant. It is a fine example of the use of polychrome bricks, which were used to decorate industrial buildings. The mill was adjacent to Kingston Dock, and the district had numerous grain mills, such as the Tradeston and Victoria Grain Mills. On 9th July 1872 fourteen workers were killed in an explosion at the nearby Tradeston Flour Mills, caused by highly explosive airborne flour dust igniting. The Kingston Grain Mills were latterly occupied by Arbuckle Smith, warehousemen. This photograph was taken in June 1975 not long before demolition in 1978. The site is now occupied by a wholesale warehouse.

The ground floor of the building at the corner of Kingston Street and West Street was once the premises of the Bank of Scotland. Further along West Street stands a grain mill, built in 1887 for J. Buchanan, grain millers, sporting a partly painted white frontage. Many industrial and commercial buildings in Glasgow changed use and ownership in their lifetimes, and this one was no exception. The North British Storage and Transit Co. Ltd. and Forth & Clyde Sack Hiring Co. became later occupants of the mill. Furthest from the camera the castellated tower of the Victoria Grain Mills, built in 1896 rises above the passing traffic.

This photograph from December 1975 shows the corner of Laidlaw Street and Wallace Street in the Kingston district of the city. The tenements are functional rather than ornate, and reflect the social class who would have lived here, namely the manual trades and their families. More ornate tenements, in what could be considered better class areas, would usually be for white collar workers. Below the wall-head chimney, we can see a line of bricked up windows. One urban myth persists that they were bricked up to reduce a 'window tax', which is not the case. Behind them are the flues or 'lums' from fires in the tenement, leading up to the chimney. The architect put 'dummy' windows here to maintain the symmetry of the design.

Above: The now gone SCWS building occupying the Paterson Street, Morrison Street and Wallace Street block displayed what a substantial organisation the Co-operative was. SCWS was founded in 1868, and became part of the fabric of everyday life. With shops and warehouses scattered around the city, it was able to provide for every need of the typical Glasgow family. Housewives would accrue dividends by shopping at the Co-op, and even today many are still able to recite their mother's 'divi' number, which was effectively the fore-runner of the modern store loyalty cards.

Below: The SCWS warehouse at 71 Morrison Street was built in 1919 on the site of a former bonded warehouse to a design by James Ferrigan. He was employed by the Co-op as an architect and had at one time worked for the prestigious practice of Honeyman, Keppie and Mackintosh. The building was used by the Grocery Department to service its many retail outlets throughout the city, and has in recent years been converted into an apartment block. To the rear, fronting on to Wallace Street was an earlier warehouse designed by Bruce & Hay, now replaced by a modern housing development.

Below: The Co-op has provided a 'cradle to the grave' service for the citizens of Glasgow, everything from christenings, clothes for the school years, venues and catering for weddings, right through to end of life funeral services. The inscription above the door at the Laidlaw Street and Wallace Street corner confirms 'This Memorial Stone Laid 22nd June 1889'

Above: The Morrison Street and Laidlaw Street complex of the SCWS was complemented by the substantial presence of the Shieldhall Works a few miles further west. The works were established in 1887 and as they developed over the years, became an industrial village in their own right. They housed many aspects of the large and diverse range of products and manufactured goods provided by the Co-op including soft drinks production, sauce and pickle works, boot and shoe making, cabinet making, printing and hosiery.

This ornate warehouse in Dalintober Street was completed in 1887 as part of the SCWS complex, which still dominates the landscape on the south east side of the Kingston Bridge. Designed by the architects Bruce & Hay, the warehouse was used as the fruit department, among other things. On the upper floor was the Dalintober Hall and a committee room. Dalintober Street was originally called Clarence Street, and underwent a name change like many Glasgow streets, to avoid duplication. The woman with her children are walking along Laidlaw Lane, previously known as Dundas Lane, and one of Glasgow's lesser known thoroughfares.

The main SCWS block fronting on to Morrison Street was completed in 1897 and designed by architects Bruce & Hay, and was believed to be their submitted but unsuccessful plans for the City Chambers, although denied by them at the time. The progress of the construction of the SCWS building was reportedly hampered by a lack of stonemasons in Glasgow, and costs were reduced by the committee overseeing the build by omitting what they believed to be unnecessary ornamentation. The building was adorned at the top by a female sculpted figure by James Alexander Ewing representing *Light and Life* which prompted the urban myth that it was a copy of the Statue of Liberty, gifted to the city by the USA. In 2016 a replica was sculpted by Kenny Mackay, and the 12 feet high figure, gilded in 23 carat gold leaf, once again stood atop the former SCWS building.

At 344 Paisley Road stands the Kingston Halls and Public Library, built in 1905 to a design by R.W. Horn, who was employed by the City Engineers Department of Glasgow Corporation. It is believed he modelled the building on the Athenaeum Building at West George Street. Kingston Halls were badly damaged by fire in 1948 and were later completely re-modelled. In more recent times they have been used as a night shelter for the homeless. To the left of the halls stood the Parkholm Biscuit Bakery, which dated from 1857, and is now the site of a hotel. The lane at the side of the halls is known as Parkholm Lane.

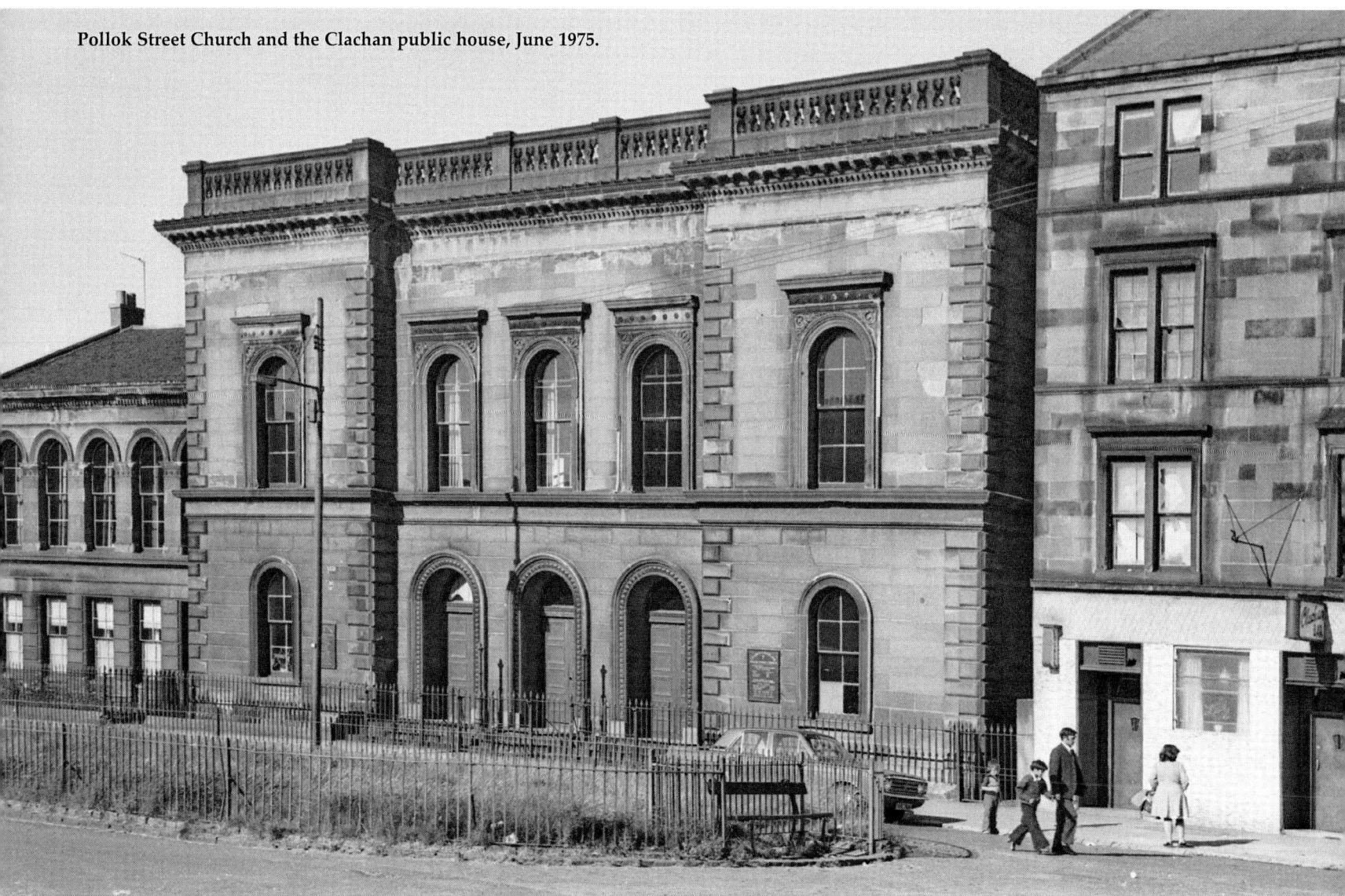
Pollok Street Church and the Clachan public house, June 1975.

This is a view, in April 1974, of the west side of Pollok Street, south of Houston Street. The street was named after the Pollok Estate and laid out around 1836, and was believed to be one of the widest streets in Glasgow. It had a centre garden area, running all the way from Paisley Road to Scotland Street, and would have made it one of the more desirable addresses in the district. Note the dormer window emerging from the roof between the chimneys. Apparently this tenement owner decided it was better to extend than move house.

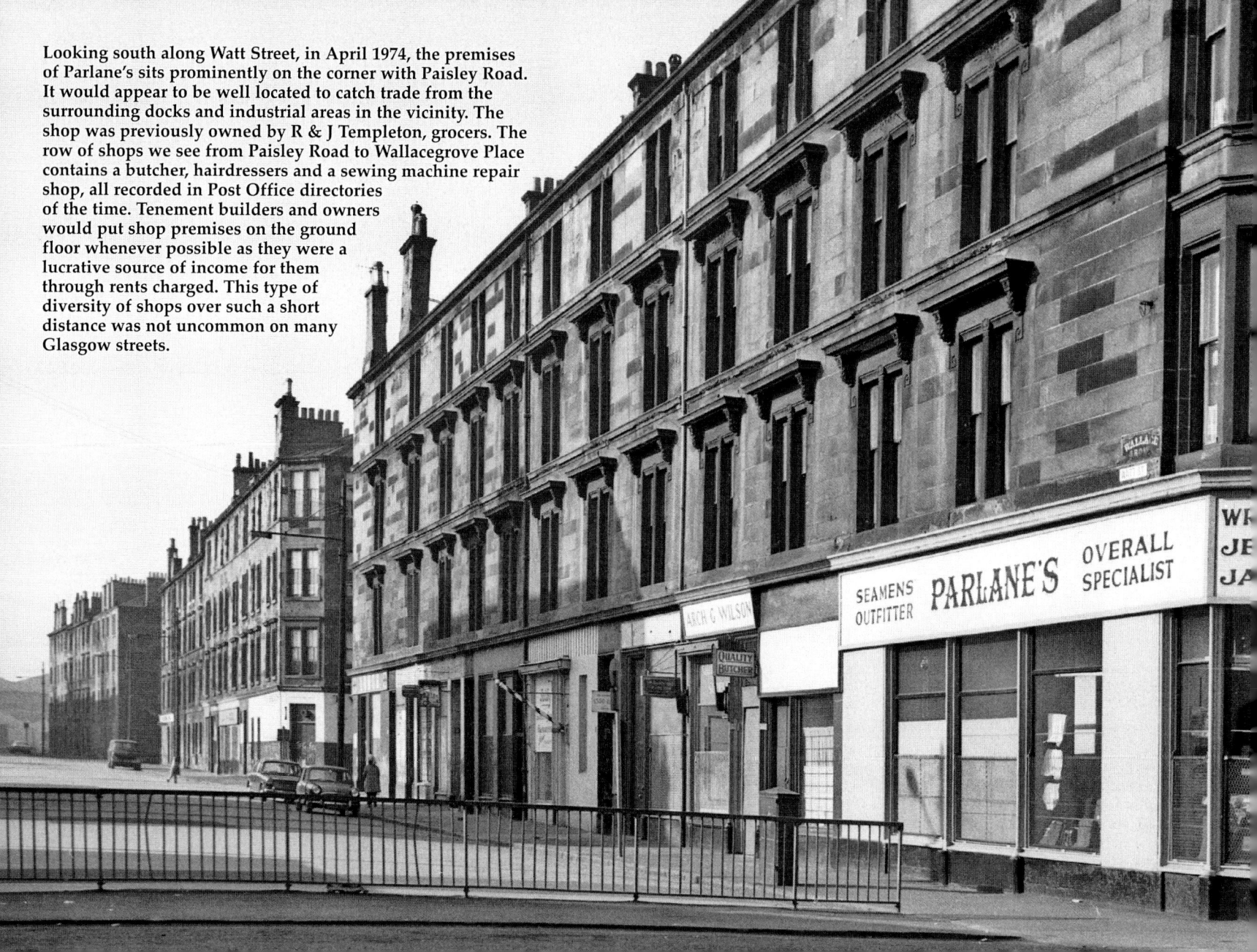

Looking south along Watt Street, in April 1974, the premises of Parlane's sits prominently on the corner with Paisley Road. It would appear to be well located to catch trade from the surrounding docks and industrial areas in the vicinity. The shop was previously owned by R & J Templeton, grocers. The row of shops we see from Paisley Road to Wallacegrove Place contains a butcher, hairdressers and a sewing machine repair shop, all recorded in Post Office directories of the time. Tenement builders and owners would put shop premises on the ground floor whenever possible as they were a lucrative source of income for them through rents charged. This type of diversity of shops over such a short distance was not uncommon on many Glasgow streets.

This view of Paisley Road taken, in April 1974, from Admiral Street has remained largely unaltered. At the No. 486 is Fergie's public house, owned by a former Rangers player, Alex Ferguson. Born at Shieldhall Road he played for a number of Scottish teams including Rangers at nearby Ibrox, but it was as a manager he was to find success, with Aberdeen and more notably Manchester United. He is rated by many as the finest manager in British football and received a knighthood in 1999. Sharing the stretch with the pub are a ladies outfitters, hairdressers and a Chinese restaurant. To the extreme left of the photograph can just be seen the edge of the Grand Ole Opry, a popular venue for Glaswegians who enjoyed country and western music. For a time the building also served as the Imperial Cinema.

The public houses of Jim Baxter and the Old Toll Bar stand like sentries at the opening that is Admiral Street, in this photograph from June 1975. Jim Baxter was well-known for his flamboyant football career, and perhaps best remembered for playing 'keepie-uppie' against England, the then World Champions, at Wembley in 1967, in a 3-2 victory for Scotland. Paisley Road Toll was the original site of Parkhouse Toll, where fees were collected from traffic travelling between Glasgow and Paisley. In 1988 the Old Glasgow Club commissioned a post to commemorate the toll, and it still stands on the north side of Govan Road opposite the Old Toll Bar. Above the public house is a dental surgery on the first floor. It is still not uncommon in Glasgow for dentists to have their practices, 'up a close' on the first floor of a tenement.

The flared trousers of the man crossing Mair Street at Paisley Road West firmly dates this image in the 1970s. Mair Street was named after John Mair who owned the Plantation Estate which stood in the vicinity, and from which the district was to take its name. The district was laid out in a grid, with Mair, Eaglesham and Plantation Streets running north to south and Craigiehall Street dissecting them at their mid point.

Occupying the corner site of Edwin Street and Clifford Lane stood Cessnock Church built in 1876 as Paisley Road United Free Church to a design by McKissack & Rowan. In the background to the right of the church stands Lambhill Public School, dating from 1876, whilst visible to the left is another church, the United Presbyterian at Cornwall Street.

Above: One of Glasgow's hidden architectural gems must surely be Walmer Crescent at Cessnock. Completed in 1862 to designs by the celebrated Alexander Thomson, it was described by local historian Brotchie as being the place of residence of 'rich merchants'. The Crescent originally enjoyed gardens to the front, but these disappeared to accommodate a row of shops fronting on to Paisley Road West. A boy with a Chopper bike and the other wearing flared trousers are iconic of the decade.

Below: As districts developed in Glasgow during the 19th century, so to did the requirement to meet the local population's spiritual needs. Plantation Parish Church opened in 1874 to a design by Robert Baldie, at 109 Plantation Street. The adjacent church hall to the right, was used by church groups most nights of the week. The church was also known as Plantation St. Andrew's Parish Church and Kinning Park Parish Church.

On the extreme left is the hazy outline of the Angel Building at Paisley Road Toll, built in 1889 to a design by Bruce & Hay, for Ogg Brothers, drapers. It later became a gent's tailors and is now a fashionable Italian restaurant. Just behind it is Toll Lane, which leads into Lauriston Lane, providing access to the rear of the impressive row fronting on to Govan Road. These townhouses are quite elegant and would have been the preserve of the better classes when they were built in the mid 19th century. At the corner of Toll Lane and 3 Govan Road is a public house, owned for many years by the Shuttleton family, and later known as the Jeanie Dean's. William Thomson & Sons sold pianos from the premises for over 50 years. Only the Angel Building remains of this view from April 1974.

Rutland Crescent was clearly built as a superior development attracting a well heeled clientele. Linking Govan Road to Paisley Road West, it was named after the Duke of Rutland and laid out around 1850. Many Glasgow streets adopted the name of English nobility. In the centre is Plantation Masonic Hall crowned with a flagpole, and for many years the meeting place of Lodge Plantation No. 581. The vacant ground to the bottom right is where Rutland Crescent School stood, built in 1883 to a design by H & D Barclay. The school closed in the late 1950s and was used as a store by Glasgow Museums before being demolished in 1969. Also to the right, Portman Street fades off into the background.

This stretch of Govan Road just to the west of Rutland Crescent would not be out of place in the West End. Occupying the corner is the gable of Rutland Crescent School, whilst adjacent are two well-appointed tenements, adorned at the top with a lattice balustrade, which later became the home of the Marine Engineers Association. By the late 1940s the property had been acquired as a schools' clinic by the Education Department. The loss of many fine buildings in Glasgow has been lamented over the years, and this image is perhaps as good an example as any of what was lost.

Facing page: By April 1974 the tenement on Govan Road and Rutland Lane was falling into disrepair and signalled that demolition was not far away. This portion of Govan Road was previously known as Rutland Place, as it was a practice in Glasgow in the late 19th century to name sections of streets by another name, usually in an attempt to 'gentrify' the address.

Eaglesham Street ran from 69 Govan Road to 138 Paisley Road West and was named after the Renfrewshire village of the same name. At Nos 7 to 11 stood the Glasgow Seamen's Friend Society, built in 1883 to a design by Clarke & Bell, to accommodate mariners in the area. The building had reading and recreation rooms and provided welfare facilities, and would have been well positioned for the nearby docks and berths. The tenement next to it enjoyed some nice features before its obvious decline. A few youngsters enjoying a game of 'fitba' seem unperturbed by their surroundings.

MacLean Street in Plantation takes its name from William MacLean who owned an estate in the area. As industrialisation gripped Glasgow in the mid 19th century, the old estates disappeared and the land was given over to industrial and housing use. In these photographs the demolition of tenements at the junction of MacLean Street and Govan Road appears to have little disregard for the safety of the passing public. The gable end of the condemned tenement still finds time to advertise rolling tobacco whilst the Chevalier public house is in its final throes in June 1975.

Facing page: This tenement at the corner of Carmichael Street and Govan Road is in a derelict condition, in February 1974, and awaits demolition with the roof cleared of slates to be sold on. At the corner was the Grand Central Bar public house, whilst some kids hang around looking for something to capture their attention.

At the corner of Vicarfield Street and Carmichael Street stands a dilapidated tenement with the Widdows public house occupying the ground floor; it was previously known as The Whitefield Vaults. The lounge appears to be separated from the main pub by the close-mouth. After the Second World War many pubs started to add lounges, which would mainly be frequented by couples, as women would not in general enter the public bars. Carmichael Street takes its name from the Carmichael family, who were the Earls of Hyndford, whilst Vicarfield Street is called after Vicarfield House which stood in the vicinity.

The unconventional architecture of Govan UP Church dates from 1870 to a design by James Thomson, and was built on the site of the former Govan United Secession Church at the corner of Copland Road and Govan Road. By June 1975 it had fallen into disrepair and awaited demolition. To the left in the background a crane serving Graving Dock No. 3 is visible.

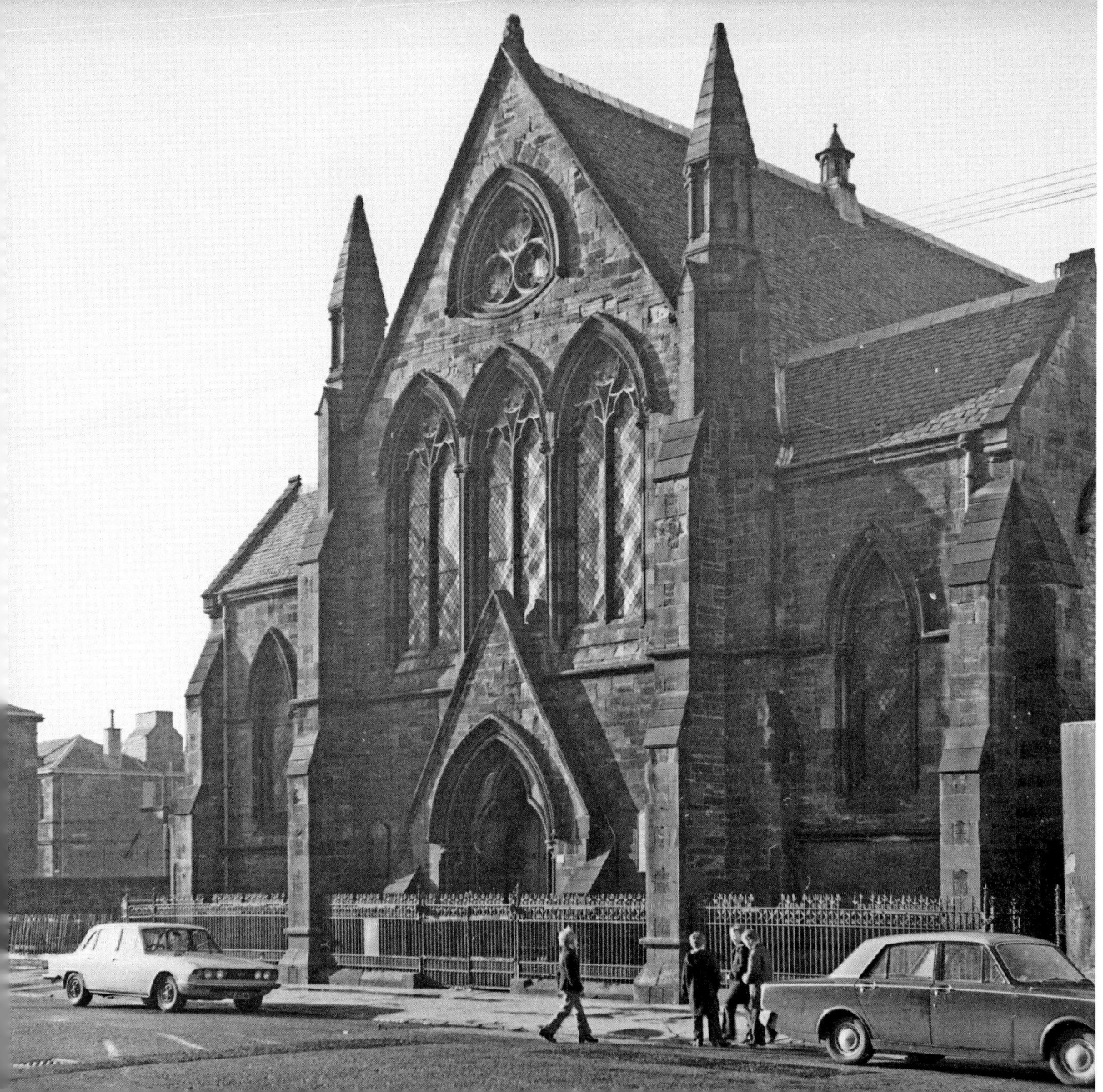

Less than a hundred yards away from Govan UP Church, stood Dean Park Parish Church dating from 1872 by the architect John Keppie. In 1932 the congregation merged with St. Kiaran's and adopted the name of St. Kiaran's – Dean Park Church. The vacant ground to the left of the church was once the site of Govan Baptist Church, built in 1876 to a design by John Honeyman. In 1888 Honeyman and Keppie formed an architectural practice that later gave a young Charles Rennie Mackintosh a job as a draughtsman. With three places of worship in such close proximity this particular part of Govan could very well have been known as 'Holy Corner'. The young lads meeting in front of the church are suitably clothed for the cold February 1974 day.

Copland Road Primary School was built in 1886 to a design by Wilson & Stewart under the auspices of Govan School Board. The original two storey school building when it opened in 1874 stood in what became the boys' playground. Early attendances at the school were affected by pupils suffering from measles and scarlet fever. The building shown was erected on the site of Victoria Cottage which was purchased for £1,350. The construction costs of the school amounted to £8,885, and it was capable of accommodating 1,045 pupils. The school log shows a female teacher being absent in 1917 having heard of the death of her third brother in the trenches of France. When the Second World War broke out many of the pupils were evacuated to Ayrshire, whilst two classrooms at the school were used by the ARP. In 1969 the school amalgamated with Broomloan Road School, and by the early 1970s was approaching its latter days.

In this view, from July 1975, looking west along Govan Road on the extreme left are the sheds of the Govan Shipbuilding Works, premises of Harland & Wolff. These were later used as the venue for productions of the plays *The Ship*, and *The Big Picnic*. The conical building in the centre is the Three Ell Corner Buildings. The narrow street between the tenements is Three Ell Lane, formerly known as Bryce Lane, and the name is believed to be derived from the fact that it was the breadth of three weaver's ells. An ell was a measurement thought to be the length of King Henry's arm, remembering Govan's weaving past.

Remaining on Govan Road, the public house in the centre was known as the Three Ell Bar, and was built on the site of a former inn run by a man called James Watson, whilst on the other corner stands Kai Johansen's pub, previously known as the Clyde Bar. Johansen was Danish by birth, and came to Glasgow to play football for Rangers. The tenement run west of Three Ell Lane was previously known as Orchard Place.

This view was taken, in February 1974, looking south along Stag Street, and in former times was part of a drovers' route, when Highlanders would bring their livestock from the north, down Crow Road at Partick where they would cross the River Clyde, which had a ford at this point. They would then continue their journey by way of Highland Lane and Stag Street, which was previously known as Maxwell Street. Local folklore says that it was around here that the last stag in Govan was killed, and indeed in the old Govan village a tavern existed called The Stag Inn.

Dock No. 1 of the Govan Graving Docks was opened in 1875 as a ship repair facility for the Clyde Navigation Trust, reflecting the development of shipbuilding and ship repair on the river. The docks were further expanded in 1886 and 1898 with new basins of almost 600 and 900 feet long. Dock No. 3, which was the longest, was constructed in mass-concrete, and ran from Stag Street to the turn in Govan Road, just past Carmichael Street, and was capable of accommodating two vessels for repair. The Graving Docks are seen here in July 1975 and remained operational until 1988.

This image taken in July 1975 shows the latter days of Nos. 574 to 596 Govan Road, or Orchard Place as it was previously known. The quality of the tenements almost seems to diminish from east to west, starting with the ornate Three Ell Corner Buildings, to a rather plain and sorry looking building at the west end. Southcroft Street branches off Govan Road and takes its name from Southcroft House which stood in the vicinity. It was owned by a banker and land agent called Thomas Baird, and for a time Southcroft Street was known as Baird Street. Leitch's Stores appears to have been an emporium offering all manner of products to the local population, although the young girls seem more interested in getting their photograph taken.

A view photographed in July 1975 of Govan Road at Southcroft Street, where a local housewife takes centre stage, complete with headscarf and message bag over her arm, a la 'Mary Nesbitt', wife of Rab, who both lived in the district in the BBC Scotland series *Rab C Nesbitt*. The offices of the Industrial Boiler Scaling Co. seem slightly out of place alongside the Stag Fish Restaurant, hairdressers and shop selling Barr's soft drinks. The little opening on the extreme left of the picture is Commons Lane, which led through to Clydebrae Street and would have been a well-used thoroughfare in old Govan village.

The three youngsters at the fountain probably have no idea who it is dedicated to. It is the Aitken Memorial Fountain, which was unveiled in 1884 and dedicated to John Aitken, who was the first Medical Officer for Govan Burgh in 1864. The fountain was cast by Cruikshank & Co., at their foundry at Denny. Aitken was a keen Freemason and active in the Order of Oddfellows; both organisations emblems adorn the fountain. In 1864 Govan was granted burgh status, and it had to go about establishing a municipal infrastructure which included burgh chambers, a police and fire service, and school board. In the background the former Bank of Scotland premises have become campaign HQ for Jeremy Thorpe's Liberal Party. There were two general elections in 1974. The first was on the 28th February, only a few weeks after this photograph was taken. Harry Selby of the Labour Party took the Govan seat from Margo MacDonald, of the SNP, who had won it the previous year at a by-election. He retained the seat in the second general election on 10th October. The Liberal candidate, Peter McMillan, came fourth in the February 1974 contest. Just visible on the right is The Govan Arms public house.

Facing page: On this stretch of the south side of Govan Road (Nos. 721 to 733) were a few remaining examples of the weavers' style cottages that were common in the area. Latterly these ones became shops and commercial premises with glaziers G & J Rae and Nicholl's Stores, who specialised in hardware trading. To the extreme right stands the Plaza Cinema, which was built in 1936 and could seat over 2,200 people. It replaced an earlier cinema on the site called the Govan Cinema, which dated from 1913 with a capacity of 1,200. Glasgow was long known as 'Cinema City' with over 120 cinemas, each changing their programmes twice per week. Very often sweet shops such as Birrell's and R.S. McColl's would open alongside, to catch some passing trade.

The rear of the cottages at 717 to 719 Govan Road are reaching the end of their useful life by February 1974.

Right: Govan Parish Church is laid out on one of the most ancient sites in the Glasgow area. It was built adjacent to Doomster Hill, which stood on the east side of Water Row and served as a 'moot hill' or 'law hill' and was pre-Christian. The original church dated from 565 A.D. and was dedicated to St. Constantine. The current church is the fourth on the site, and was completed in 1888 to a design by Edinburgh architect Sir Robert Rowand Anderson, the foundation stone having been laid by Isabella Elder. The church is known for its hog-backed stones which are believed to be Scandanavian from the 10th century. In 1996 Channel 4's Time Team programme carried out an archaeological dig at the church and nearby Doomster Hill.

Below: The final resting place of Thomas Baird of Southcroft House in Govan Parish Churchyard looks slightly out of place against the panorama in the background. In the centre is the spire of the University of Glasgow at Gilmorehill, where it moved to from High Street in the mid 19th century. To the right, high above the Clyde and the Kelvin stands Yorkhill Hospital, with the modern ward buildings looking quite imposing. Some historians believe the Romans had a camp at Yorkhill, and strategically that would be easy to understand. The warehouses of Scotway Haulage in Castlebank Street have now been demolished as part of the Clydeside Expressway re-alignment and Glasgow Harbour Development.

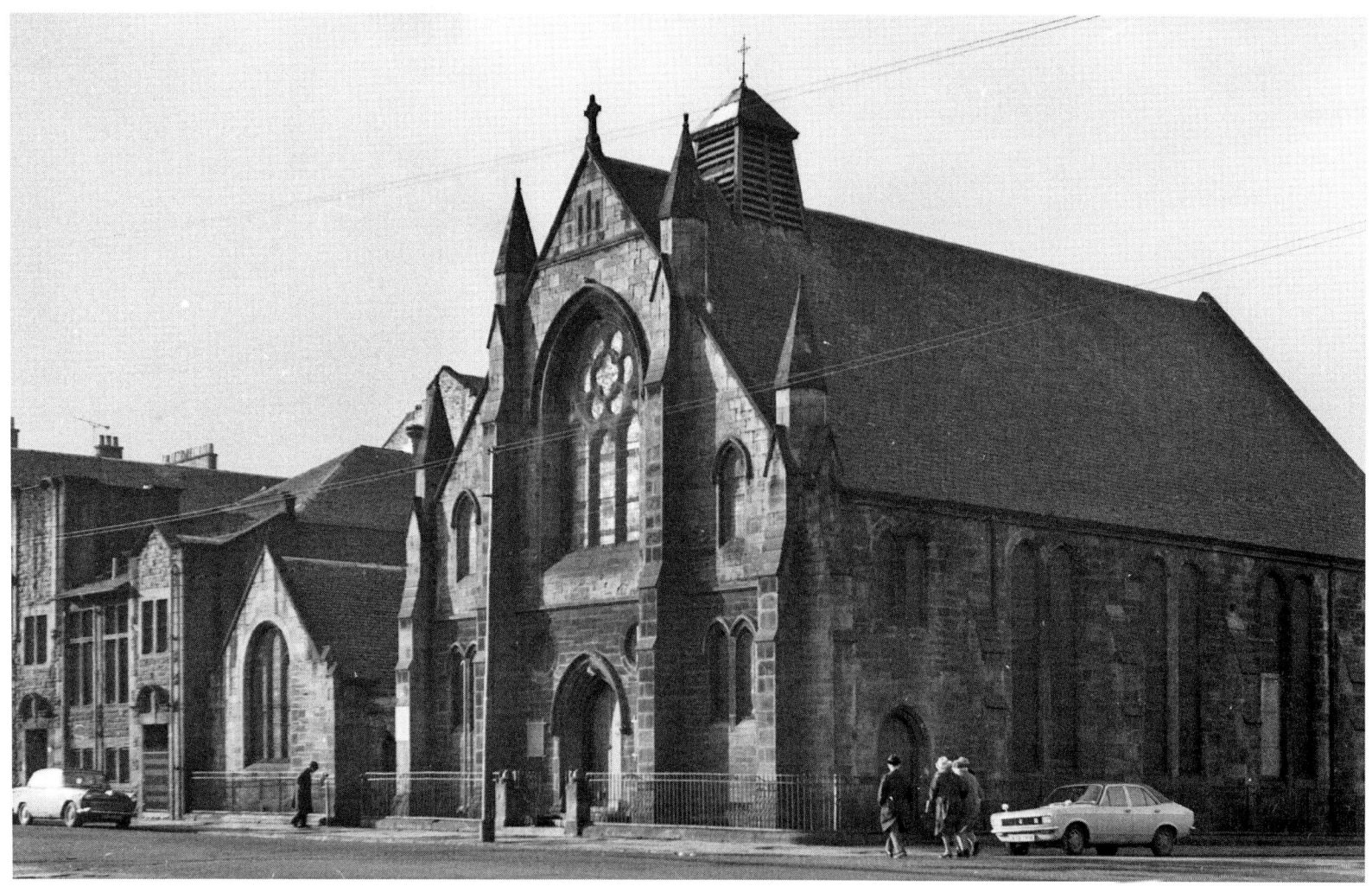

It would appear that God was never far from Golspie Street. At the corner with Fairfield Street at No. 30 stood Fairfield U.F. Church which dated from 1882. At No. 36 and to the left is the Salvation Army Citadel, which opened in 1904. Wedged between the two is the church hall. Golspie Street was originally known as White Street, and also contained another place of worship, at No. 106, Elder Park Parish Church from 1884. Further along, at No. 112, is the Gladstone Memorial Institute of 1906.

Looking south along Golspie Street from the Langlands Road junction the spire of Govan Parish Church, built in 1886, dominates the scene. It was also known as Elder Park Parish Church. Beyond it the gable elevation of a tenement run, and the public baths at Harhill Street are visible. The corner tenement at Langlands Road bears a date of 1872. The Boar's Head public house occupies a prime spot for thirsty travellers. In the foreground the public telephone box (a K6 or kiosk type 6) is from the pre mobile phone era, when not everyone had a home telephone, and would have to use a public box to make their calls. Golspie Street continues into the distance and where it crosses Helen Street it becomes a little cul-de-sac known as Belch Street.

Elder Park Parish Church takes its name from the nearby Elder Park, which was gifted to the people of Govan by Isabella Elder, wife of John, the shipbuilder. Her generosity is well-documented and as well as the park she also helped fund the Elder Library and the Chair of Naval Architecture at the University of Glasgow. Being something of a feminist, she gifted Queen Margaret College for the further education of women and helped establish a training home for nurses. She is remembered by a statue located appropriately in Elder Park, the first statue of a woman in Glasgow with the exception of Queen Victoria.

A working boat heads upstream passing the yard of Fairfield at Govan, a centre of shipbuilding on the Clyde. In 1834 Charles Randolph began manufacturing engines at Tradeston, and in 1852 he was joined by John Elder with the aim of building ships. In 1858 they took over the Govan Old Shipyard together with a neighbouring site called Fairfield, and the firm of the same name was established. Fairfield pioneered the compound engine which, with its growing reputation, ensured a full order book, and it became a main player in the heyday of Clyde shipbuilding. Following the Geddes Report of 1966 shipyards on the Clyde at Glasgow and Clydebank were amalgamated to form Upper Clyde Shipbuilders, bringing together John Brown's, Connell's. Stephen's and Fairfield's yards. The former Fairfield yard was to go to experience several changes of ownership in the years that followed and now trades under the BAE banner. To the left of the yard was a children's swing-park.

The latter days of the Clyde as a vibrant working river with cargo ships being loaded and unloaded. To the right is the vessel *Daghestan*, an ore carrier over 500 feet long and built in 1960 by Harland & Wolff at Govan for the Hindustan Steam Shipping Company Limited of Newcastle. It was later named the *Lovinda* and then the *Mercury* before being scrapped in Turkey following an engine fire.

This view was taken from Water Row at Govan looking towards the north bank of the Clyde with the Western Infirmary, the tower of Glasgow University and the Sick Children's Hospital at Yorkhill completing the skyline. It was from Water Row that the Govan Ferry ran, crossing the river to Ferry Road, with the first ferry shuttling between Govan and Pointhouse in 1734. The service from Water Row came under the management of the Clyde Navigation Trust in 1857 before being finally withdrawn in 1965.